The Book of Coding

A Practical Guide to Teenagers

Abeer Verma

Fusion Books

Publisher : **Fusion Books**
X-30, Okhla Industrial Area, Phase-II
New Delhi-110020
Phone : 011- 40712200
E-mail : wecare@diamondbooks.in
Website : www.diamondbooks.in
Edition : 2026

AUTHOR'S NOTE

When I first started learning to code, I thought it was about memorizing commands and typing strange symbols correctly. But very quickly, **I realized something important:**

Coding is not about syntax.
It's about thinking.
It's about breaking a problem into smaller parts.
It's about asking, "What happens next?"
It's about finding patterns and improving step by step.

Every app we use, every website we visit, every game we play — runs on code written by someone who once started with the basics. This book is written for teenagers who want to move beyond just using technology and begin understanding how it works. I've tried to explain coding in a way that feels clear, practical, and realistic — without overwhelming jargon.

You don't need to be a genius to code.
You need curiosity, patience, and consistency.
If this book helps you build your first working program — and understand why it works — then it has done its job.
Let's build something meaningful.

— Abeer Verma

Preface

Why Coding Matters Today

We live in a world powered by software.
From social media platforms and banking apps to healthcare systems and space exploration — coding drives innovation across every industry.

But coding is not only about technology careers. It builds logical thinking, structured problem-solving, creativity, and resilience — skills that are valuable in every field.

The Big Book of Coding – A Practical Guide for Teenagers is designed to:

• Explain programming fundamentals clearly
• Develop logical and algorithmic thinking
• Encourage hands-on experimentation
• Teach debugging as a skill, not a frustration
• Introduce real-world applications of coding
• Provide a foundation for future learning

Rather than presenting coding as a complex technical subject, this book approaches it as a practical skill — something you can build step by step.

Coding is not about writing perfect programs the first time.
It's about learning through iteration and improvement.
As technology continues to evolve, the ability to understand and create software will become one of the most empowering skills of this generation.
This book is your starting point.

Foreword

In the 21st century, coding has become a new form of literacy. Just as reading and writing empowered earlier generations, the ability to understand and create software empowers today's students.

Coding teaches more than programming. It develops:

- Logical thinking
- Structured reasoning
- Precision in communication
- Patience in problem-solving
- Confidence in experimentation

The Big Book of Coding stands out because it emphasizes clarity and application. It encourages teenagers to not only learn programming concepts but to build, test, debug, and improve — mirroring the real-world development process.

By focusing on fundamentals and practical understanding, this book prepares young learners not just for exams, but for a future shaped by technology.

Coding is not about replacing creativity.
It is about amplifying it.
May this book inspire students to think structurally, solve confidently, and build responsibly in a digital world.

Contents

Chapter 1

What Is Coding, and Why Should I Care?

Introduction: Let's Decode "Coding"

Have you ever asked Siri a question, played a game like Minecraft, ordered food online, or scrolled endlessly on Instagram? If yes, then guess what—you've been using the magic of coding all along!
Coding, also known as programming, is the art of telling computers what to do. Just like we speak different languages like Hindi, English, or Tamil to communicate with each other, we use special languages called programming languages to communicate with computers.
At its core, coding is about solving problems using logic and giving machines step-by-step instructions to get something done.

Let's take an example:
You want a robot to brush your teeth. You can't just say, "Hey robot, go brush my teeth!"

You'll have to give exact instructions:

1. Walk to the sink.
2. Pick up the toothbrush.
3. Open the toothpaste cap.
4. Squeeze toothpaste.
5. Brush teeth in circular motion for 2 minutes.
6. Rinse mouth.

See? That's what coding looks like—clear, logical, step-by-step instructions.

Real-Life Analogy: Coding is Like a Recipe

Imagine you're baking a cake. The recipe says:

- Take 2 cups of flour.
- Add 1 cup of sugar.
- Mix with eggs and milk.
- Bake for 30 minutes at 180°C.

You follow the recipe to make a yummy cake. Similarly, a computer follows your "code" to complete a task—like playing music, solving a maths problem, or opening a website.

Where Do We See Code in Everyday Life?

We live in a digital world, and almost everything around us is powered by code.

Let's spot a few examples from your daily routine:

Daily Action	How Code Is Involved
Unlocking phone with Face ID	AI-based code matches your face
Watching YouTube	Code streams video from servers
Google Maps	Code finds shortest route & traffic updates
Scanning QR to pay	Code handles transactions securely
Typing in WhatsApp	Auto-correct and emojis are coded features
Playing BGMI or Free Fire	Game engines use thousands of lines of code

Even our homes are getting smarter—with smart fans, smart bulbs, and voice assistants like Alexa—all of them run on code.

Why Should YOU Learn Coding?

Let's be real. Coding might sound technical or geeky, but it's one of the most important and fun skills you can learn today.

Here are 5 rock-solid reasons:

1. It Builds Logical Thinking
Coding trains your brain to solve problems in steps, just like solving a puzzle or playing chess. It sharpens your analytical thinking.

2. It Boosts Creativity
Want to build your own game or design a website? With coding, your ideas come to life. You're not just a user—you become a creator.

3. It Leads to Cool Careers
Software Developer, Game Designer, AI Engineer—the tech world is booming, and skilled coders are in demand globally.

4. It Helps in Other Subjects Too
Coding improves your performance in math, science, and even language subjects. It helps you think clearly and explain better.

5. It Makes You Future-Ready
In a world run by AI, automation, and digital tech, coding is the language of the future. It opens up opportunities in every industry—from health to space.

Busting the Myths: Coding Isn't Only for Geniuses

Let's clear some common myths about coding:

Myth	Truth
"You need to be a math topper."	Nope! Coding is more about logic and thinking. Math helps, but it's not a must.
"Only boys are good at it."	Completely false! Coding is for everyone—girls, boys, artists, thinkers, storytellers.
"It's boring and full of numbers."	No way! You can create music, build games, animate stories, and more through code.
"You need to be 18+ to start."	You can start at any age—even 5-year-olds use Scratch to code stories.

Fun Example: Code in Action (Game Edition)

Let's say you want to build a mini-game where:
- A monkey collects bananas.
- Every time it jumps and catches a banana, the score increases.
- The game ends when the monkey misses 3 bananas.

To build this game, you'd:

1. Draw the characters (monkey and bananas).
2. Define movements (jumping, falling).
3. Set conditions (if banana caught, score++; if missed, lives--).
4. Add a loop (game keeps going till 3 lives lost).
5. Show final score.

All these steps are done using code. And yes, you can build it using simple block-based tools like Scratch!

Try This: Code Without Code!

Here's a fun challenge. Write down how you brush your teeth as step-by-step instructions.

Example:
1. Go to the bathroom.
2. Pick up the toothbrush.
3. Squeeze toothpaste.
4. Brush top teeth (10 seconds).
5. Brush bottom teeth (10 seconds).
6. Rinse mouth.
7. Keep brush back.

Congratulations! You've just written your first algorithm—no computer required!

Code is the Superpower of the Digital World

Think of your smartphone. It's made up of:
- A screen
- A battery
- Buttons
- A processor

But what makes it smart is the software—apps, settings, camera filters, security, reminders. And that software is written using code.

Without code, a phone is just a box of metal and plastic. With code, it becomes your best friend, tutor, calculator, entertainment system, and fitness tracker—all in one.

How India is Powering the Tech World

India is already a global tech hub. Major Indian companies like:
- Infosys
- TCS
- Wipro
- Zoho
- Byju's

...all run on software.

And Indian minds are leading global companies too!
- Sundar Pichai (CEO of Google)
- Satya Nadella (CEO of Microsoft)
- Arvind Krishna (CEO of IBM)

You could be next.

Thought Experiment

You're the PM of a digital-first India. What problem would you solve with coding?

Here are some ideas:
- Traffic jams?
- School homework reminders?
- Water saving sensors?

Design your dream app. Give it a name. What does it do?
Think. Sketch. Plan. That's how tech entrepreneurs start.

Coding is Not Just for IT Companies

You might think coding only matters in tech companies. That's not true!

Here's where coding is being used:

Field	How Coding Helps
Agriculture	Soil health tracking, weather alerts
Healthcare	AI for disease diagnosis
Entertainment	Animation, CGI in movies
Space	Satellites, Mars missions, ISRO projects
Education	e-Learning platforms like Byju's, Vedantu

Teen Coders Who Built the Future

Tanmay Bakshi

Started coding at 5. Now a Google AI expert and motivational speaker at 18.

Harshita Arora

Built a cryptocurrency tracking app. Got featured by Apple and Forbes. She was just 16.

Shraddha Sharma

Started a music channel at 15. Used tech to build her audience and now runs her own platform.

What do they all have in common? They started small. Stayed curious. Kept building.

What Will You Build?

The journey of every coder begins with curiosity.

Start asking:

• What's behind this app?
• How does this game work?
• Can I make something better?

Once you start asking, you'll start learning, building, and eventually leading.

Abeer's Coding Insight

Coding becomes easier when you stop seeing it as complex commands and start seeing it as structured thinking. Every program follows logic — and logic is something you already use daily.

Quick Recap

Let's summarize what you've learned in this chapter:

• Coding is giving instructions to a computer to do tasks.
• You see code everywhere: phones, games, AI, banks, schools.
• Coding builds logical thinking, creativity, and future-ready skills.
• Anyone can learn coding—not just toppers or engineers.
• The world needs more thinkers, dreamers, and doers—like YOU.

Self-Check: Quiz Time!

1. What is coding in one sentence?
2. Name two places where code is used in your daily life.
3. What is an algorithm?
4. Can a student with no math background learn coding?
5. What's one app/game idea you'd love to build?

Activity

Draw a comic strip where a robot is confused because you didn't give it clear instructions. Then, rewrite the steps properly. This shows how coding needs precision.

Bonus Tip

Install Scratch or visit scratch.mit.edu and explore the beginner games. Try changing colors, characters, or messages.
You've taken your first real step into the world of coding!

Chapter 2

The Language of Computers

Programming Basics

Introduction: Computers Don't Speak Hindi or English!

Have you ever tried talking to your computer or phone like a person? If you say, "Hey computer, do my maths homework," nothing happens. That's because computers don't understand human language. They only understand very specific, logical instructions written in a format they can process—this is called code.

But here's the interesting part: just like humans have different languages (Hindi, Tamil, English, Marathi), computers also have many programming languages! Each has its own rules, grammar (called syntax), and special powers.

This chapter will introduce you to the languages of computers, so you can start "talking" to them in their own words!

What is a Programming Language?

A programming language is a set of words, symbols, and rules used **to write instructions for computers. It helps us:**

- Tell the computer what to do
- Control how a program behaves
- Build software, games, websites, and apps

Think of it like a recipe book written in computer-friendly language.

High-Level vs. Low-Level Languages

There are two major types of computer languages:

Type	Description	Example
Low-Level	Close to how computers work (more technical, harder to read)	Assembly, Machine Code
High-Level	Easy for humans to read and write	Python, JavaScript, Java, C++

For beginners, we use high-level languages because they're simpler and look more like English.

Frontend vs. Backend: The Two Sides of an App

When you open an app or website, two things are happening behind the scenes:

Frontend	Backend
What users see	What makes it work
Buttons, colors, layout	Login system, saving data, sending emails
HTML, CSS, JavaScript	Python, Java, Node.js, PHP

Think of a food delivery app:
• Frontend = what you see (menu, restaurant list)
• Backend = what you don't see (order tracking, payments, delivery mapping)
Both are important and work together like a team.

Let's Meet Some Popular Programming Languages

Here are the top languages every teen coder should know about:

1. Python
• Easiest for beginners
• Looks like English
• Great for AI, automation, data analysis
Example:
python
CopyEdit
```
print("Hello, world!")
```

2. HTML/CSS
• Used to design web pages
• HTML = content; CSS = design
Example:
html
CopyEdit
```
<h1>Hello!</h1>
<style>h1 {color: red;}</style>
```

3. JavaScript
• Adds movement and logic to websites
• Makes pages interactive (e.g., buttons, games)
Example:
javascript
CopyEdit

alert("Welcome to my website!");

4. Java

- Used in Android apps and large systems
- More structured, used by companies

5. C++

- Powerful, fast, and great for games
- A bit more complex, but worth learning later

Basic Building Blocks of Coding

Just like grammar in English, every programming language has basic elements.

Let's understand the most important ones:

1. Variable

A container to store data. Like a school bag holds books, a variable holds numbers, words, or values.

python
CopyEdit

```
name = "Aman"
age = 15
```

2. Loop

A repeating action. Great for tasks that happen again and again.

python
CopyEdit

```
for i in range(5):
    print("Hi!")
```

("Hi!" will print 5 times)

3. If-Else Statement

Used for decision making. **Like:**

- If it's raining, carry an umbrella.

• Else, wear sunglasses.

python
CopyEdit
```
if age >= 18:
    print("You can vote")
else:
    print("Too young to vote")
```

4. Function

A block of code that performs a task. Think of it as a mini-program.

python
CopyEdit
```
def greet():
    print("Hello there!")
```

5. Syntax

Every language has grammar. In code, it's called syntax. If you miss a comma or bracket, it will cause an error.

6. Bug

A mistake in code that causes problems. Debugging is fixing the bug!

Tools of the Trade – IDEs

To write and run your code, you need an IDE (Integrated Development Environment). It's like a notebook + spell-check + test zone all in one.

IDE	What It's Good For
VS Code	Most popular among students
Replit	Online coding with friends
Thonny	Great for Python beginners
Scratch	Drag-and-drop coding for fun games

Coding Box: “Hello World” in 3 Different Languages

Let’s print “Hello World”—the first thing every coder learns:

Language	**Code**
Python	print(“Hello World”)
JavaScript	console.log(“Hello World”);
HTML	<p>Hello World</p>

Simple, right? You’re already writing code!

Let’s Compare: Natural Language vs. Code

Natural Language	**Programming Code**
“Turn on the fan”	fan.on()
“Add 2 and 3”	print(2 + 3)
“Say Hello”	print(“Hello”)

Just like learning to speak takes practice, learning to code is about trying, testing, and improving.

Mini Challenge: Guess the Output!

What will this code do?

python

CopyEdit

```
for i in range(3):
    print(“Coding is cool!”)
```

Try running it on replit.com or in Thonny.

Answer:

It prints “Coding is cool!” three times!

Why Do Different Languages Exist?

Just like we have different tools for different jobs (pen for writing, hammer for fixing), different programming languages are made for different needs:

Language	Best For
Python	AI, data science, automation
JavaScript	Interactive websites
HTML/CSS	Web page structure & design
Java	Android apps, enterprise software
C++	Game engines, system software

Over time, you'll discover which one fits your interest best.

Recap Table

Concept	Meaning
Variable	Stores data
Loop	Repeats actions
If-Else	Makes decisions
Function	Reusable block of code
Syntax	Code grammar
Bug	Error in code

Career Corner: Who Uses These Concepts?

- Game Designers use loops and functions to control characters
- Web Developers use HTML/CSS/JS to build websites
- AI Engineers use Python to train machines to think
- Cybersecurity Experts use all languages to find and fix system vulnerabilities

Everything starts from these basics.

Thought Experiment

If you could teach your computer one thing, what would it be?

Examples:
- Automatically wish friends “Happy Birthday”
- Organize your homework files
- Tell you when to take a break from scrolling reels

Write the steps for how it would work. Congrats—you just drafted your first program idea.

Chapter Summary

Let’s review what you’ve learned:
- Programming languages help you “talk” to computers.
- High-level languages (like Python) are easy and beginner-friendly.
- Frontend = What you see; Backend = What makes it work.
- Learn the basic elements: variables, loops, if-else, functions.
- Practice writing simple code and understanding the output.

Quiz Time

1. What is the difference between high-level and low-level languages?
2. What are variables used for?
3. Which language is best for creating websites?
4. What does a “loop” do in coding?
5. Name one IDE used to write code.

Abeer’s Coding Insight
If you can explain your solution clearly in plain language, you can code it. Always write the logic on paper before typing it into a compiler.

Try It Yourself – Activity

Open replit.com, create a free account, and:
1. Choose Python.

2. Type:

python
CopyEdit
name = input("What's your name? ")
print("Welcome, " + name + "!")

3. Run the code and type your name.
You've just created your first interactive program!

Chapter 3

Problem Solving & Logical Thinking

Introduction: More Than Just Code

You've now learned how to write your first few lines of code. But before you become a coding master, you must unlock the most important superpower of a good programmer: problem-solving. Coding is not just about writing lines of code—it's about solving real-world problems using logic, creativity, and clarity.
Whether it's building an app, debugging an error, or designing a game—every coding journey begins with breaking down a problem into simple steps.
This chapter will teach you how to think like a computer scientist—step by step, decision by decision.

What Is Problem Solving?

In coding, problem-solving means creating a solution using logic and code. **It involves:**

1. Understanding what needs to be done
2. Breaking it into smaller steps
3. Figuring out the best way to solve each step
4. Turning those steps into code

It's like being a detective—analyzing clues, asking questions, trying out solutions, and fixing errors until everything works.

Real-Life Analogy: Making Maggi Noodles

Let's say you want to make a bowl of Maggi.

Here's what your brain does (problem-solving in action):
1. Boil water
2. Add noodles
3. Add tastemaker
4. Cook for 2 minutes
5. Serve hot

That's a step-by-step algorithm! And that's exactly what coders do—write down the steps for the computer to follow.

Step 1: Understanding the Problem

Let's say the task is:
"Find the biggest of 3 numbers."

Before jumping into code, ask yourself:
- What's the input? (Three numbers)
- What's the output? (The biggest number)
- What do I already know? (Comparisons like > or <)
- What's the goal? (Print the largest number)

This is the first step: clearly understanding the problem.

Step 2: Break It Down

We call this decomposition—breaking a big problem into tiny steps.

For our example:

1. Ask the user for 3 numbers
2. Compare the numbers
3. Find which is largest
4. Print the result

Suddenly, the problem doesn't feel scary, right? That's the power of breaking it down.

Step 3: Think Logically

To compare numbers, you need logic. In coding, we use:

- If-else statements: to make decisions
- Boolean values: true or false
- Operators: like >, <, == (equal to), != (not equal to)

So, if you want to check:

python

CopyEdit

```
if a > b:
   print("A is bigger")
```

Logical thinking is like asking yes/no questions to reach the answer.

Step 4: Turn the Steps into Code

Now let's write the actual Python code:

python

CopyEdit

```
a = int(input("Enter first number: "))
b = int(input("Enter second number: "))
c = int(input("Enter third number: "))
```

```
if a >= b and a >= c:
   print(a, "is the largest")
elif b >= a and b >= c:
   print(b, "is the largest")
else:
   print(c, "is the largest")
```

You just solved your first logic-based coding problem!

Mini Challenge: Reverse a Word

Problem: Take a word from the user and print it backwards.

Break it down:

1. Input a word
2. Reverse it
3. Print the reversed word

Python Code:

python

CopyEdit

```
word = input("Enter a word: ")
reversed_word = word[::-1]
print("Reversed:", reversed_word)
```

Easy, right?

What Are Algorithms?

An algorithm is a list of clear, ordered instructions to solve a problem.

It's like giving directions:

- Go straight for 100m
- Turn left at the temple
- Stop at the blue gate

In coding:

- Each line is a step
- The goal is clear
- The logic flows step-by-step

Example algorithm: Find even or odd number

1. Take a number as input
2. Divide it by 2
3. If remainder is 0 → Even
4. Else → Odd

Flowcharts – Drawing Your Thinking

A flowchart is a diagram that shows the steps of a problem as shapes and arrows.

Shape	Meaning
Rectangle	Step (e.g., print, input)
Diamond	Decision (e.g., if yes/no)
Oval	Start/End

Here's a simple flow:

css

CopyEdit

```
[Start] → [Input number] → [Check if number % 2 == 0?]
  Yes → [Print Even]
  No → [Print Odd]
→ [End]
```

You can draw flowcharts on paper or online tools like draw.io or Lucidchart.

Activity: Algorithm for Making Tea

Write down the steps for making tea. **Your list might look like:**
1. Boil water
2. Add tea leaves
3. Add sugar and milk
4. Let it simmer
5. Strain into cup
6. Serve hot

This is your tea-making algorithm. Now think: What if you had to teach this to a robot?

You'd need:
- Exact steps
- Correct order
- Clear instructions

Just like in coding!

Debugging: Fixing Mistakes

Even with perfect planning, errors (bugs) happen. That's okay!

Here's how to fix them:
1. Read the error message – Python is pretty helpful!
2. Check your code – Typos, indentation, or missing brackets?
3. Use print() – Print values to check what's going wrong
4. Test small parts – Break big code into smaller testable chunks
5. Ask for help – Google, Stack Overflow, or ChatGPT!

Debugging is a skill that improves with practice—don't fear errors; learn from them.

Try It Yourself: Make a Simple Calculator

Task: Add, subtract, multiply or divide two numbers.
Steps:

1. Ask user to enter two numbers
2. Ask for operation (+, -, *, /)
3. Perform the operation
4. Show result

Python Code:

python
CopyEdit

```
a = float(input("Enter first number: "))
b = float(input("Enter second number: "))
op = input("Choose operation (+, -, *, /): ")

if op == "+":
    print("Result:", a + b)
elif op == "-":
    print("Result:", a - b)
elif op == "*":
    print("Result:", a * b)
elif op == "/":
    print("Result:", a / b)
else:
    print("Invalid operation")
```

Boom—you've built a mini calculator!

Pattern Recognition – Spot the Logic!

Problem-solving also means looking for patterns.
Example: Find square numbers from 1 to 10
Python:

python
CopyEdit

```
for i in range(1, 11):
    print("Square of", i, "is", i*i)
```

Here, you noticed a pattern: square = number × number. That's how coders think—spot → apply → automate.

Real-World Problem Solving with Code

Problem	Code Solution
Need reminders	Make a task app
Lost files	Write an organizer script
Forget birthdays	Build a birthday alert bot
Long shopping list	Make a grocery app

You're not just learning code—you're learning how to solve problems smartly.

Bonus Project: Number Guessing Game

```
python
CopyEdit
import random
num = random.randint(1, 10)
guess = int(input("Guess the number (1 to 10): "))

if guess == num:
    print("Correct! ")
else:
    print("Wrong! The number was", num)
```

Concepts used:

- Random number
- Input/output
- Condition checking

Challenge: Add chances or loops to retry!

Quick Recap

Concept	Meaning
Algorithm	Step-by-step instructions
Flowchart	Visual map of logic
Debugging	Finding and fixing code errors
Decomposition	Breaking problems into smaller parts
Pattern recognition	Spotting repeatable logic

Logical thinking Making smart decisions using if, else, loops

Quiz Time

1. What is an algorithm?
2. How is a flowchart useful?
3. What does if-else help you do in code?
4. What is debugging?
5. Can you name one real-world problem that coding can solve?

Activity – Your Own Algorithm

Task: Write an algorithm for packing your school bag.

Example:
1. Check timetable
2. Add books for each subject
3. Pack pencil box and notebook
4. Add tiffin and water bottle

Then write this as a flowchart!

Abeer's Coding Insight
Think of variables as labeled boxes. When you understand what goes inside each box, half of coding confusion disappears.

Final Thoughts

In the world of coding, tools change, languages evolve—but logical thinking will always be your superpower. Whether you're building a calculator, solving a puzzle, or automating a boring task, logic is your best friend.

Every great coder—from Steve Jobs to the student coder next door—started with simple problem-solving. So practice daily, break things down, build your logic, and grow step by step.

Chapter 4

Building with Blocks – Visual Programming

Introduction: Code Without Typing? Yes, Please!

Imagine building your own game or animation—not by typing lines of confusing code, but by simply dragging and dropping colorful blocks on a screen. Sounds fun, right?
Welcome to the world of visual programming, where you code by stacking blocks instead of writing text. It's like building with LEGO—but instead of castles, you're building programs!
This chapter will help you discover how visual programming tools like Scratch and MIT App Inventor make it easy and exciting to start coding—even if you've never written a single line before.

What is Visual Programming?

Visual programming is a way to program using graphical blocks instead of text. Each block represents a command, loop, or logic—

and you just fit them together like puzzle pieces.
Instead of worrying about spelling or syntax errors,

you focus on:
• Understanding the logic
• Seeing the output instantly
• Building things with creativity and fun

It's perfect for beginners, kids, artists, and even adults who want to make their first app or game without learning a complex language.

Why Visual Programming Is Great for Beginners

Advantage	Why It Matters
No syntax errors	You don't need to remember commas or brackets
Drag-and-drop interface	Super easy to learn and use
Immediate results	See your animations or games in real time
Fun and interactive	Great for creative projects
Builds logical thinking	Teaches the foundation of real coding

Visual programming is a stepping stone to learning real-world programming languages like Python or JavaScript later.

Meet Scratch: The Superstar of Block Coding

Scratch is a free, online visual programming platform created by MIT. It's used by millions of students around the world.

Website: https://scratch.mit.edu

Scratch lets you:
• Animate characters (called sprites)

• Make your own stories and cartoons
• Build fun games and quizzes
• Share your creations with a community

You don't need to install anything—just open the website and start creating!

Getting Started with Scratch – Step by Step

Step 1: Go to scratch.mit.edu
Click "Create" to open the Scratch editor.

Step 2: Meet the Stage and Sprite
• Stage = Where your story/game appears
• Sprite = The character (like the cat) you control

Step 3: Explore Block Categories
Blocks are grouped into categories:
• Motion (move, turn)
• Looks (say, change color)
• Sound (play sound, meow!)
• Events (start when clicked)
• Control (repeat, wait, if-then)
• Sensing (touching, mouse position)

Step 4: Drag and Drop Your First Code
Try this:
1. Drag "when green flag clicked"
2. Add "say Hello!"
3. Click the green flag above the stage

Your sprite talks!
Now add a motion block:
• "move 10 steps" — your sprite moves on the stage!

Example: Make a Sprite Dance

1. When green flag clicked
2. Repeat 10 times:
   o Turn 15 degrees
   o Move 10 steps
3. Add a "meow" sound

You've just created your first animated sequence!

Behind the Blocks – What's Really Happening?

Each block you use in Scratch is secretly doing what real code does:

- Loops like repeat → for/while loops in Python
- Conditions like if → if-else statements
- Variables → same as storing values in any language

So while you're playing with blocks, you're training your brain for real coding.

Try This Mini Challenge: Sprite Quiz

Make a quiz that asks a question and checks the answer.
Steps:
1. Use "ask [What is 2+2?] and wait"
2. Use "if <answer = 4> then [say Correct!] else [say Try again!]"

That's if-else logic, visually!

MIT App Inventor – Build Android Apps with Blocks

Want to make your own app for your phone? Try MIT App Inventor!
Website: https://appinventor.mit.edu
It's another block-based platform—but this one lets you build Android apps that you can actually install and use.

You can build:

• A click-counter app
• A voice translator
• A quiz app
• A flashlight app
• And even games!

Getting Started with App Inventor – Step by Step

Step 1: Go to appinventor.mit.edu
Click "Create apps!" and sign in with your Google account.

Step 2: Designer View
This is where you design your app layout:

• Add buttons, labels, images, sliders
• Drag them onto your mobile screen

Step 3: Blocks View
Now click "Blocks" tab.

• Use blocks to tell your app what to do
• Example: "when Button1.Click → set Label.Text to 'Hello'"

Step 4: Connect Your Phone
Use the MIT AI2 Companion App to test your app live on your phone via a QR code.

You've built your first mobile app without typing a single line of code!

Project Idea: Tap Counter App

1. Add a Button labeled "Tap me!"
2. Add a Label to show the count
3. In blocks view:
    o Use a variable for count

o When button is clicked → count = count + 1
o Update label with new count

This teaches you:
• Variables
• Event handling
• Updating UI dynamically

Game On: Build a Clicky Game in Scratch

Create a game where a sprite moves and the player has to click on it.
Steps:
1. Randomly move the sprite every second
2. Use the "when sprite clicked" block
3. Increase score by 1 every time clicked
4. Add sound and animation

Game elements:
• Loops
• Variables (score)
• Events (click)
• Conditions (win/lose)
You just made your first interactive game!

Creative Ideas with Blocks

Idea	Platform	What You'll Learn
Make a talking pet	Scratch	Sound + animation
Daily mood app	App Inventor	UI + data storage
Multiplication quiz	Scratch	Conditions + math
Step counter app	App Inventor	Sensors
Magic 8-ball fortune teller	Scratch	Random numbers

Your imagination is your only limit!

What Can You Build With Block Coding?

Project Type	Examples
Games	Maze runner, Pong, shooting gallery
Stories	Comic strips, interactive books
Music	Soundboard, beatboxer
Learning Tools	Quiz apps, math puzzles
Useful Apps	To-do list, translator, reminder app

Each of these projects can become a portfolio piece or even a school science fair entry.

Visual Programming Builds Real Skills

While it's fun and easy, visual programming builds powerful skills like:

- Problem-solving
- Logical thinking
- Sequencing
- Creativity
- Debugging

And it makes the transition to real code much smoother later on.

Real vs. Visual Programming – A Comparison

Feature	Scratch / App Inventor	Python / Java
Uses blocks	✔	✗
No syntax errors	✔	✗
Fast to learn	✔	✗
Good for creativity	✔	✔
Great for careers	(starter)	(pro-level)

Best for	Beginners, kids, artists	Advanced learners, job-seekers

Use visual programming to build confidence, then move to real code when ready.

Resources to Explore More

Resource	Platform	What You Can Learn
Scratch Studio	scratch.mit.edu	Projects by other teens
CS First by Google	csfirst.withgoogle.com	Themed Scratch activities
App Inventor Gallery	appinventor.mit.edu	Real apps built by students
Hour of Code	code.org	Visual coding games
Tynker	tynker.com	Visual + text-based coding

Explore, remix, and create your own versions!

Chapter Recap

Let's review what we learned in this colorful chapter:

- Visual programming means coding using blocks instead of text
- Scratch helps you create games, animations, and stories easily
- MIT App Inventor helps you build real Android apps with no typing
- You learn the same logic as real code: loops, conditions, variables
- It's fun, creative, and the best way to start if you're new to coding

Quick Quiz

1. What is the name of the main character in Scratch?
2. What does the “when green flag clicked” block do?
3. Name one app you could build using MIT App Inventor.
4. Which block category helps you make decisions in Scratch?
5. What is the difference between the Designer View and Blocks View in App Inventor?

Abeer’s Coding Insight
Most programs are just decisions and repetitions. If you master “if” and “loops,” you can build almost anything basic.

Activity – Design Your First Block Project

1. Pick a topic: a quiz, game, story, or utility app
2. Choose a platform: Scratch or App Inventor
3. Write 3 features your project will have
4. Draw a rough sketch of how it will look
5. Start building!

Example: A “daily motivation” app that shows a new quote every time you click a button.

Chapter 5

From Web to Wow – Learn HTML, CSS & JavaScript

Introduction: The Magic Behind Every Website

Every time you open YouTube, Google something, or scroll through Instagram, you're using the web. But have you ever wondered what makes these websites look and work the way they do?

The answer is three powerful tools:

HTML, CSS, and JavaScript—the holy trinity of web development. This chapter will introduce you to these three technologies, help you build your very first webpage, and unlock the creative world of frontend web development. By the end, you'll be able to say, "Yes, I built that website!"

The Foundation of the Web

Here's how web development works:

Language	What It Does
HTML (HyperText Markup Language)	Structure – the content of your page
CSS (Cascading Style Sheets)	Style – how your page looks
JavaScript	Behavior – how your page responds to users

Let's use a real-world analogy:

• HTML is the skeleton – it builds the bones of the page (text, images, layout).

• CSS is the clothes and makeup – it makes the page pretty and stylish.

• JavaScript is the brain – it adds interaction like buttons, pop-ups, games.

What Does a Basic Web Page Look Like?

Let's create your first HTML page!

html

CopyEdit

```
<!DOCTYPE html>
<html>
  <head>
    <title>My First Web Page</title>
  </head>
  <body>
    <h1>Hello, world!</h1>
    <p>This is my very first web page.</p>
  </body>
</html>
```

Let's break it down:

- <!DOCTYPE html> – tells the browser it's an HTML5 document
- <html> – the entire webpage
- <head> – info about the page (not visible)
- <title> – name that shows in the browser tab
- <body> – where your actual content goes

Save the file as index.html and open it in your browser. You'll see your web page!

Activity: Create Your Own Bio Page

Use this template:

html

CopyEdit

```
<!DOCTYPE html>
<html>
  <head>
    <title>About Me</title>
  </head>
  <body>
    <h1>Hi, I'm Ananya!</h1>
    <p>I love coding, drawing, and playing football.</p>
    <p>My favorite food is pizza.</p>
  </body>
</html>
```

Edit the name, hobbies, and food. Save and refresh the browser. Boom! You just built a website.

Add Style with CSS

HTML is nice but plain. Let's make it pop with CSS.

There are 3 ways to use CSS:

1. Inline – inside a tag
2. Internal – inside <style> in the head
3. External – separate .css file (for bigger projects)

Let's use internal CSS for now.

html

CopyEdit

```
<head>
  <style>
    body {
      background-color: #f0f8ff;
      font-family: Arial;
    }
    h1 {
      color: darkblue;
    }
    p {
      font-size: 18px;
      color: #333;
    }
  </style>
</head>
```

Now your site has color, fonts, and style!

Try It Yourself: Make a Styled Profile Page

Steps:

1. Create an HTML file
2. Add a <style> section
3. Style your headings and paragraphs
4. Add background colors, borders, and padding

CSS lets you be a digital artist.

Time to Make It Move: JavaScript

JavaScript (JS) adds life to your webpage.

With JS, you can:

- Show alerts
- Make buttons do things
- Change content
- Create games and animations

Let's write a simple JS alert:

html

CopyEdit

```
<script>
  alert("Welcome to my awesome site!");
</script>
```

Add this inside your <body> and reload the page. You'll see a popup greeting!

Let's Add a Button with JavaScript

html

CopyEdit

```
<button onclick="sayHello()">Click Me!</button>

<script>
  function sayHello() {
    alert("Hello from JavaScript!");
  }
</script>
```

This does two things:

- Adds a clickable button
- Triggers a JS function when clicked

You just built interaction!

Project: Build a Mini Interactive Webpage

Combine all 3:

html

CopyEdit

```
<!DOCTYPE html>
<html>
<head>
  <title>My Interactive Page</title>
  <style>
    body { background-color: #fefbd8; text-align: center; }
    h1 { color: teal; }
    button { padding: 10px; font-size: 16px; }
  </style>
</head>
<body>
  <h1>Welcome to My Web World</h1>
  <p>Click the button to get a surprise!</p>
  <button onclick="alert('You are awesome!')">Click Me</button>
</body>
</html>
```

Save it as fun.html and run it in your browser. Simple + colorful + interactive!

How the Web Works (Simplified)

1. You write HTML/CSS/JS code
2. Save it on your computer or upload it to the internet
3. A browser (like Chrome or Firefox) reads your code and displays it
4. Other people can now access your page online!

To go live, you'll later learn about:

- Hosting platforms (GitHub Pages, Netlify)
- Domain names
- Responsive design for mobile devices

Build Your Skills with These Projects

Project	What You'll Practice
Personal Bio Page	HTML, headings, paragraphs
My Hobbies List	Lists, images
Favorite Quotes	CSS styling, fonts
Simple Quiz Game	JavaScript buttons + logic
Color Changer	JS + CSS + user events

Each of these can be done with just a browser and a text editor!

Activity: Make a Favorite Movie Website

Your goal:

- Create an HTML page
- Add movie name, image, short review
- Style it with CSS
- Add a JS button to reveal your rating

Advanced:

- Add multiple movies using <div> sections
- Use JS to sort or filter

Tools to Code Your Website

Tool	Use
Notepad / Notepad++	Basic text editor for HTML
VS Code	Free and powerful editor for all coding
Replit	Online IDE (no install needed)
CodePen.io	Try HTML/CSS/JS in your browser
GitHub Pages	Free website hosting for your projects

No fancy setup needed—you can build a website in 15 minutes!

What's the Difference?

Language	Purpose	Example
HTML	Structure	<h1>Title</h1>
CSS	Style	h1 { color: red; }
JavaScript	Behavior	alert("Hi!")

Together, they build the modern web.

Real-World Uses of HTML, CSS, JS

Industry	Example
E-commerce	Amazon pages with buttons, filters
Education	Online quiz apps, e-learning tools
Social Media	Instagram stories and posts
News & Blogs	Scroll animations, layout design
Gaming	Browser-based games using JS

By learning these skills, you can build your own digital creations.

Teen Coders Who Built Cool Web Stuff

• Aanya, 16 – Built a "Study Tracker" app using HTML and JS for her class
• Kartik, 17 – Created a blog for his science club using Replit and GitHub Pages
• Meenal, 15 – Designed an interactive "Poetry Showcase" for school fest
If they can do it, so can you.

Chapter Recap

Let's review what we covered:
• HTML = structure of a webpage
• CSS = style and design
• JavaScript = interactivity and logic
• Together, they power every website you use daily
• You can build your first webpage with just a few lines
• Platforms like CodePen, Replit, VS Code help you build faster

Quick Quiz

1. What does HTML stand for?
2. Which tag is used to make the largest heading?
3. How do you change text color in CSS?
4. What is JavaScript used for in a webpage?
5. Name one platform where you can write and run HTML/CSS/JS online.

Abeer's Coding Insight
Good coders don't write everything at once. They break problems into small reusable parts. That's how real software is built.

Final Activity: Build Your Own Portfolio Homepage

1. **Use HTML to add:**
   - o Your name
   - o A short bio
   - o Projects list
2. **Use CSS to:**
   - o Add background colors
   - o Style fonts and headings

3. **Use JavaScript to:**
   - o Add a "Contact Me" button
   - o Show an alert with your email/phone

Save it. Show it. Improve it. This is your first step into becoming a web developer!

Chapter 6

Learn Python

The Best First Language

Introduction: Meet Python – Your Friendly First Language

If coding languages were superheroes, Python would be the cool, calm, and super-smart hero everyone wants to learn from.
Why?

Because Python is:
• Easy to read ✔
• Easy to write ✔
• Powerful and widely used ✔
• Great for beginners AND pros ✔
From building games and websites to running artificial intelligence and space missions, Python is the most versatile and in-demand programming language today.
Let's dive into Python and start writing code you'll actually understand and enjoy!

Why Python is Beginner-Friendly

Reason	Why It's Great
Simple syntax	Looks like English
Versatile	Used in AI, web, games, automation
Huge community	Millions of coders to learn from
Tons of tutorials	Easy to find help online
Popular in schools	CBSE, NEP 2020 recommend it

Python lets you focus on logic, not grammar. That's why it's often the first language taught at Google, MIT, and even NASA!

Your First Python Code – Step by Step

You can write and run Python code in:

• Online editors like Replit

• Offline IDEs like Thonny or VS Code

Let's begin with the classic:

python

CopyEdit

```
print("Hello, world!")
```

This simple line:

• Tells Python to display a message

• Uses the print() function

• Doesn't need semicolons or curly braces like other languages

Congratulations—you've just written your first Python program!

Activity: Say Hello to Yourself

python

CopyEdit

```
name = input("What is your name? ")
```

print("Hi, " + name + "! Welcome to Python.")

This introduces:

- input() – takes user input
- Variables – store data (like name)
- + – joins strings (text)

Try different names and see what changes!

Python Basics You Must Know

Let's break down the most important building blocks:

1. Variables

Think of variables as containers that store information.

python

CopyEdit

age = 15

language = "Python"

Python automatically understands whether it's a number or text.

2. Data Types

Type	**Example**
Integer (int)	age = 14
Float (decimal)	pi = 3.14
String (text)	name = "Aarav"
Boolean (True/False)	is_cool = True

3. Loops

Loops repeat actions. **Two main types:**

For Loop:

python

CopyEdit
for i in range(5):
  print("Practice makes perfect!")
While Loop:
python
CopyEdit
x = 1
while x <= 3:
  print(x)
  x += 1

4. If-Else Conditions

Used for decisions.
python
CopyEdit
age = int(input("Enter your age: "))
if age >= 18:
  print("You can vote!")
else:
  print("Too young to vote.")

5. Functions

Functions are reusable blocks of code.
python
CopyEdit
def greet():
  print("Hello, there!")
greet()

6. Lists

A list stores multiple values.
python

```
CopyEdit
fruits = ["apple", "banana", "mango"]
print(fruits[1])  # Outputs: banana
```

You can loop through lists:

```
python
CopyEdit
for fruit in fruits:
    print(fruit)
```

Project 1: Number Guessing Game

```
python
CopyEdit
import random
num = random.randint(1, 10)
guess = int(input("Guess the number (1-10): "))

if guess == num:
    print("Correct! ")
else:
    print("Oops! The number was", num)
```

Concepts used:

- import a module
- random.randint()
- if-else

Project 2: Simple Calculator

```
python
CopyEdit
a = float(input("Enter first number: "))
b = float(input("Enter second number: "))
op = input("Choose operation (+, -, *, /): ")
```

```
if op == "+":
    print(a + b)
elif op == "-":
    print(a - b)
elif op == "*":
    print(a * b)
elif op == "/":
    print(a / b)
else:
    print("Invalid operation")
```

Concepts used:

- Variables
- Conditionals
- Math operations

Project 3: Quiz Game

python

CopyEdit

```
score = 0
answer = input("What is the capital of India? ")
if answer.lower() == "delhi":
    print("Correct!")
    score += 1
else:
    print("Oops! It's Delhi.")

print("Your Score:", score)
```

Concepts used:

- Input/output
- Case handling (.lower())
- Score keeping

Debugging: What to Do When Code Breaks

Don't worry about errors—they happen to everyone!

Here's how to fix them:

1. Read the error message – Python explains it
2. Check spelling and indentation – Python is strict about spacing
3. Use print() to test variables
4. Google the error – chances are, others had the same issue
5. Stay calm – debugging is part of learning

Try These Mini Challenges

Challenge	Concepts Practiced
Odd or even checker	If-else
Multiplication table generator	Loops
Rock-paper-scissors game	Input + logic
Story generator	String + input
Countdown timer	Loops + time module

Python in the Real World

Python is used in:

- Web development (Django, Flask)
- Artificial intelligence (TensorFlow, scikit-learn)
- Data science (pandas, NumPy)
- Automation (scripts, bots)
- Game development (Pygame)

It powers companies like:

- Google
- Instagram
- Netflix

• Spotify
• NASA

Real Teen Coders Using Python

• Divya (16) built a chatbot for her school library
• Raghav (17) made a Python game and uploaded it on GitHub
• Isha (15) used Python to analyze weather data for a science fair
Python is a powerful tool even in young hands.

Tools to Practice Python

Tool	What It Does
Replit	Online coding without setup
Thonny	Simple offline IDE
Python.org	Download official version
Google Colab	Write Python in your browser
HackerRank / CodeChef	Practice coding challenges

Recommended Resources

• **YouTube:** Apna College, CodeWithHarry
• **Books:** "Python Crash Course", "Automate the Boring Stuff with Python"
• **Websites:** W3Schools, Programiz, Real Python
Explore these to go from beginner to builder.

Chapter Recap

Let's summarize what we've learned:
• Python is a simple, readable, and powerful language
• You can use it to build games, quizzes, calculators, and more
• Master the basics: variables, loops, if-else, functions, and lists

- Start small, make mistakes, and learn by doing
- Python is used by professionals across industries—from AI to apps

Quick Quiz

1. What is the output of print(3 * 4 + 2)?
2. What does input() do?
3. How do you create a function in Python?
4. What is a list? Give an example.
5. Name one platform where you can write and test Python online.

> **Abeer's Coding Insight**
> The best programmers are not those who avoid errors — they're the ones who stay calm and read the error message carefully.

Final Activity: Build a Daily Motivation App

1. Create a list of 5 motivational quotes
2. Use random.choice() to pick one quote
3. Print it with a cheerful message

Example:

python
CopyEdit

```
import random
quotes = [“You got this!”, “Keep going!”, “Believe in yourself!”]
print(random.choice(quotes))
```

Try building on this: add timers, user input, or more quotes!

Chapter 7

Real Projects You Can Build

Introduction: From Learner to Creator

You've now learned Python, web basics, logic, and visual programming—but how do you bring all of that together?
The answer: Build projects!
Projects are where learning meets doing. They make your skills real, your learning visible, and your confidence soar.
This chapter is packed with 10 fun, useful, and beginner-friendly coding projects you can build using what you already know. Whether you want to impress your friends, submit a class assignment, or start a coding portfolio—this is your launchpad.

Why Building Projects Is So Important

Benefit	**Why It Matters**
Reinforces learning	You apply what you've learned
Boosts creativity	You design your own solutions

Builds confidence	You see real results
Teaches problem-solving	You learn how to debug and adapt
Great for portfolio	Perfect for school, college, internships

Remember: You don't need to be an expert to build real stuff. You just need to start.

Project Ideas for Teen Coders

Let's explore 10 exciting projects. For each one, we'll look at:

- What it does
- What you'll need
- Which concepts you'll apply
- Bonus tips to expand it

1.To-Do List App (Python or Web)

What it does:
Lets users add, view, and mark tasks.
Tools: Python (console-based) or HTML/CSS/JavaScript
Concepts: Lists, loops, conditionals, input/output

Sample (Python):

python
CopyEdit

```
tasks = []
for i in range(3):
    task = input("Add a task: ")
    tasks.append(task)

print("Your Tasks:")
for t in tasks:
    print("- " + t)
```

Bonus: Add "mark as done" or use localStorage in JS for browser apps.

2. Rock-Paper-Scissors Game (Python or JavaScript)

What it does:
Plays the classic game against the computer.
Tools: Python or browser-based JS
Concepts: Conditionals, random, input/output

python
CopyEdit
```python
import random
user = input("Rock, Paper, or Scissors? ").lower()
choices = ["rock", "paper", "scissors"]
comp = random.choice(choices)

print("Computer chose:", comp)
if user == comp:
   print("It's a tie!")
elif (user == "rock" and comp == "scissors") or \
     (user == "paper" and comp == "rock") or \
     (user == "scissors" and comp == "paper"):
   print("You win!")
else:
   print("You lose.")
```

Bonus: Add score tracking or a best-of-5 mode.

3. Digital Clock (HTML + CSS + JavaScript)

What it does:
Displays the current time in real time.
Concepts: DOM, JavaScript Date object, styling

HTML:
html
CopyEdit
```
<h1 id=”clock”></h1>
```
JavaScript:
javascript
CopyEdit
```
function updateClock() {
  let now = new Date();
  document.getElementById(“clock”).innerText = now.
toLocaleTimeString();
}
setInterval(updateClock, 1000);
```

Bonus: Add date, background color based on time of day, or AM/PM format.

4. Quiz Game (Python or Scratch)

What it does:
Asks questions and gives a score.
Concepts: Input, if-else, score variables

Python Example:
python
CopyEdit
```
score = 0
q1 = input(“Capital of France? “)
if q1.lower() == “paris”:
   score += 1
print(“Your score:”, score)
```

Bonus: Add more questions, difficulty levels, or use Scratch for visual design.

5. Budget Tracker (Python or App Inventor)

What it does:
Tracks your expenses and shows totals.
Concepts: Variables, input, arithmetic
Python Logic:

```
python
CopyEdit
expenses = []
for i in range(3):
   amt = float(input("Enter expense: ₹"))
   expenses.append(amt)
print("Total Spent: ₹", sum(expenses))
```

Bonus: Categorize expenses (food, travel), or use App Inventor for a mobile version.

6. Weather App (HTML + CSS + JS + API)

What it does:
Displays weather using an online API.
Concepts: Fetching data, using APIs, DOM manipulation
Tools: OpenWeatherMap API, JS fetch()

Bonus: Add city search, icons, or use user location.

7. Dice Roller (Python or JS)

What it does:
Simulates rolling a dice.
Concepts: Random, output, events

```
python
CopyEdit
import random
print("You rolled a", random.randint(1, 6))
```

Bonus: Add images of dice faces or roll two dice at once.

8. School Time Table Generator (Python or HTML)

What it does:
Displays your weekly class schedule.
Concepts: Lists, tables, loops, conditionals

Bonus: Let the user customize it or add reminders.

9. Feedback Form (HTML + CSS)

What it does:
Collects user name, email, and comments.
Concepts: Form inputs, styling

HTML:
html
CopyEdit
```
<form>
  <input type=”text” placeholder=”Your name”>
  <input type=”email” placeholder=”Email”>
  <textarea placeholder=”Comments”></textarea>
  <button type=”submit”>Submit</button>
</form>
```

Bonus: Add JS to validate or style confirmation messages.

10. Compliment Generator (Python or JS)

What it does:
Displays a random compliment

Python:

```python
python
CopyEdit
import random
compliments = ["You're awesome!", "Great job!", "Keep going!"]
print(random.choice(compliments))
```

Bonus: Turn it into a daily app that sends reminders.

Think Like a Builder

Before starting any project, ask:

- What do I want this to do?
- What inputs will it need?
- What outputs will it give?
- What's the best way to structure it?

Draw it out first. Then start coding step by step.

Organize Your Projects

Create folders:

```
markdown
CopyEdit
/MyProjects
   /ToDoApp
   /QuizGame
   /PortfolioSite
```

Save all files clearly:

- index.html
- style.css
- main.py
- script.js

Keep backups online using GitHub or Google Drive.

What Makes a Good Beginner Project?

Quality	Why It Helps
Simple idea	Easier to start and finish
Visual result	See your progress immediately
Can be expanded	Add features later
Uses what you know	Builds confidence
Solves a problem	Feels meaningful

You don't need to build the next Instagram. Start with something small, finish it, and build from there.

Improve, Share, Repeat

Once you finish a project:
1. Test it – find bugs
2. Improve it – add new features
3. Share it – show friends, upload to GitHub or a blog
4. Repeat – build your next one!

Every coder grows this way.

Chapter Recap

Let's review the highlights:
• Real projects help solidify coding knowledge
• You can start with small apps using Python, HTML, JS, or Scratch
• You don't need perfection—just a clear idea and the courage to try
• There are endless project possibilities: games, tools, calculators, websites
• Keep building, improving, and sharing

Quick Quiz

1. What's one reason building projects is important?
2. What language would you use to make a quiz game?
3. What is random.choice() used for?
4. How do you organize multiple projects on your computer?
5. Name one project you'd like to start this week.

Abeer's Coding Insight
Building even a small working project teaches more than reading ten theory chapters. Always build something — even if it's simple.

Final Activity: Your First Custom Project

Plan your own project:
- Name of the project:
- What it will do:
- Which language you'll use:
- One cool feature you'll try to include:

Sketch it, plan it, then start building!

Chapter 8

Coding in the Age of AI

Introduction: Welcome to the AI Era

From Alexa answering your questions to Netflix recommending your next show and Google Photos recognizing your face—Artificial Intelligence (AI) is everywhere.
But how does it all work?
Code.
At the heart of AI are powerful algorithms, built by coders like you.
In this chapter, you'll discover how coding and AI are connected, how you can start exploring AI projects, and how Python becomes your best friend when diving into the world of intelligent machines.
Get ready to meet the future—and start building it.

What Is Artificial Intelligence?

Artificial Intelligence (AI) is when machines are programmed to think, learn, and make decisions like humans.
It's like giving your computer a brain.

AI helps machines:
• Recognize images (face unlock)
• Understand speech (voice assistants)
• Play games (chess bots)
• Recommend content (YouTube, Spotify)
• Drive cars (self-driving tech)

AI is changing healthcare, education, agriculture, business, space exploration, and beyond.

How Is AI Related to Coding?

Just like any program, AI runs on code. But there's one big difference:

Regular Code	**AI Code**
You give instructions	You give examples
Fixed output	Learns patterns and improves
Example: calculator	**Example:** face recognition

To build AI, you need to:
• Write code (mostly in Python)
• Feed data (numbers, images, text)
• Train the model (machine learning)
• Test and improve

What is Machine Learning?

Machine Learning (ML) is a type of AI where computers learn from data without being told exactly what to do.

For example:
• Show a machine 1,000 pictures of cats and dogs
• It "learns" the patterns (ears, fur, size)

• It can now guess if a new picture is a cat or dog

This process involves:

1. Data Collection
2. Data Cleaning
3. Model Training
4. Testing & Improving

All powered by—you guessed it—Python code.

Python Tools for AI Beginners

Python is the top language for AI. Here are popular libraries:

Library	Use
NumPy	Math and number crunching
pandas	Organizing and analyzing data
scikit-learn	Machine learning made simple
matplotlib	Drawing charts and graphs
TensorFlow	Deep learning and neural networks
OpenCV	Image processing and computer vision

You'll learn some of these as you grow. Start with NumPy and pandas.

Try It Yourself: Predict the Average

Let's simulate a mini AI task using Python's average function.

python

CopyEdit

```
import numpy as np

marks = [88, 76, 90, 85, 92]
average = np.mean(marks)
```

```
print("Predicted average:", average)
```

This shows how AI can learn from numbers (like student scores).

Project: Mood Detector with Teachable Machine

Not ready to code from scratch? Try Teachable Machine by Google.
Website: https://teachablemachine.withgoogle.com

It lets you:

- Train your own AI in 5 minutes
- Use your webcam, mic, or images
- No coding needed

Steps:

1. Choose a project (image/sound/pose)
2. Add training examples
3. Train the model
4. Export it to use in your website or Scratch

Try building a mood detector or gesture game controller!

What Is ChatGPT?

You're using it right now!
ChatGPT is a powerful AI model that understands and generates human-like text.

It was trained on billions of words and now helps:

- Answer questions
- Write code
- Create stories
- Summarize research
- Build chatbots

And yes—it runs on Python too!

Activity: Make a Mini Chatbot

Use this simple Python code:

python
CopyEdit

```
name = input("What's your name? ")
print("Hi " + name + "! How can I help you today?")
question = input("Ask me something: ")
print("Hmm... I'm still learning. But that's a great question!")
```

Try expanding this chatbot with more responses or greetings!

Canva AI and Creative Tools

AI is not just for coding—it's also in art and design.

Tools like:

- Canva AI – Generates text, images, logos
- DALL•E – Turns text into images
- Lumen5 – Makes videos from blogs
- Runway ML – AI for video editing and special effects

AI is now helping creators, writers, artists, and even entrepreneurs!

Cool Beginner AI Project Ideas

Project	Tools	Concepts
Emoji predictor	Python, if-else	Conditions, input
Face filter	OpenCV	Image recognition
Spam email detector	pandas + ML	Text classification
Language translator	Google API	API, requests
Number predictor	scikit-learn	Data patterns

Responsible Coding: AI + Ethics

AI is powerful—but with great power comes responsibility.

Think about:
• **Bias:** Is your data fair?
• **Privacy:** Are you protecting user data?
• **Safety:** Can your code be misused?
• **Transparency:** Can users trust your AI?

As a young coder, you have the chance to build ethical, inclusive, and safe AI tools.

How India Is Using AI

India is becoming a global AI leader with initiatives like:
• **AI for All:** Free online AI courses by CBSE & Intel
• **Smart farming:** AI-based crop analysis
• **AI in healthcare:** Early disease detection
• **AI in governance:** Chatbots for public services

By 2047, AI will be a core part of India's Digital Vision—and you could be building it.

Glossary Time

Term	Meaning
AI	Machines that mimic human intelligence
Machine Learning	Training machines using data
Model	A trained program that makes predictions
Dataset	A collection of data for training/testing
Bias	Unfair preference in training data
Python	The most popular AI coding language

Chapter Recap

Let's summarize this futuristic chapter:
• AI is everywhere—from phones to hospitals
• Python is the go-to language for AI and ML
• You can build beginner AI projects using tools like Teachable Machine
• Libraries like NumPy and scikit-learn make AI possible
• Ethics matter—AI must be used responsibly
• India's digital future includes YOU and your AI ideas

Quick Quiz

1. What is AI in simple words?
2. Name one Python library used in machine learning.
3. What does Teachable Machine do?
4. Why is ethics important in AI?
5. What's one way India is using AI today?

Final Activity: Plan an AI Project

Think of a real-world problem you'd like to solve using AI.

Use this template:
• **Problem:** (e.g., forgetting homework)
• **Idea:** (e.g., smart reminder app)
• **Input:** (e.g., schedule)
• **Output:** (e.g., notifications)
• **Tools:** Python, AI API, or Teachable Machine
Draw it out. Then try building a small prototype or demo.

Chapter 9

How to Learn Coding the Smart Way

Introduction: Work Smarter, Not Harder

Learning to code can sometimes feel overwhelming. So many languages, so many tutorials, so much jargon.

But here's a secret:
you don't need to learn everything—you just need to learn smart. This chapter is your guide to mastering coding without burning out.

You'll learn:
- Where to start
- What to focus on
- How to avoid distractions
- Which platforms to trust
- And how to keep going when things get tough

Let's unlock smarter, faster, and more fun ways to learn coding!

Start With a Plan

Before jumping into a tutorial, take a pause.

Ask yourself:

- Why do I want to learn coding?
- What do I want to build? (Websites, games, apps, AI?)
- How much time can I give each week?

Once you answer these, build a plan.

Here's a sample for a beginner:

Week	Focus
1	Python basics: print, variables, input
2	Loops, if-else, lists
3	Simple projects: calculator, quiz
4	Web dev basics: HTML, CSS
5	JavaScript intro + DOM
6	Final project (portfolio page or game)

Even 30 minutes a day can make a difference if you're consistent.

Free vs. Paid Courses – What's Best?

There are hundreds of resources—but not all are equal. Here's how to choose:

Type	Pros	Cons
Free	No cost, great for beginners	Sometimes lacks depth
Paid	Structured, in-depth, certificates	Can be expensive

Best Free Platforms

Platform	Strength
W3Schools	Learn HTML, CSS, JS step by step
Khan Academy	Visual JavaScript and logic
Code.org	Beginner-friendly block + text coding
freeCodeCamp	Full web dev + certification
Sololearn	Mobile learning + quizzes
NPTEL (India)	Govt.-backed, in-depth CS courses

Best Paid Platforms

Platform	Highlights
Udemy	Affordable courses by experts
Coursera	University-level certificates
Coding Ninjas	Popular in India, beginner to pro
WhiteHat Jr / BYJU'S Future School	1-on-1 lessons for younger students
Scaler Academy	Advanced learners, job-focused

Start with free tutorials. If you're serious later, pick one paid course to go deep.

How to Learn Efficiently

Here's your smart learning toolkit:

1. Code Along, Don't Just Watch
Typing code while watching helps you learn faster.

2. Practice Daily
Even 20 minutes a day builds muscle memory.

3. Use Pen & Paper for Logic
Before coding, write your logic like steps or flowcharts.

4. Make Your Own Notes
Create a cheat sheet for loops, syntax, functions.

5. Build Mini Projects
Apply what you learn every week.

Avoid These Common Traps

Trap	Fix
Watching 10 tutorials and doing none	Stick to one, apply it
Copy-pasting code without understanding	Pause and understand each line
Giving up after 1 error	Google it, ask help, retry
Comparing yourself to others	Your journey, your pace

Remember: Even expert coders get stuck. Progress is better than perfection.

Active Learning > Passive Watching

Passive Learning	Active Learning
Watching a video	Typing code yourself
Reading an article	Solving a challenge
Copying code	Building your own version
Memorizing	Understanding why it works

Every time you type code, break it, and fix it—you're getting smarter.

Use the "Learn, Build, Repeat" Cycle

This 3-step cycle keeps you growing:

1. Learn a new concept (e.g., loops)
2. Build something small using it (e.g., table generator)
3. Repeat with a new concept (e.g., functions)

This turns theory into real skill.

Gamify Your Learning

Make coding fun by turning it into a game!

Platform	How It Helps
CodeCombat	Learn Python/JS through fantasy games
HackerRank	Solve problems, earn stars
Codewars	Level up with challenges
Edabit	Beginner-friendly puzzles

Set goals:

- "I'll solve 5 problems this week"
- "I'll build one new project every Sunday"

Reward yourself when you succeed!

Best YouTube Channels for Teen Coders

Channel	Focus
Apna College	Hindi + clear Python and DSA
CodeWithHarry	Everything from web to AI in Hindi
BroCode	Fun, fast tutorials for all levels
Tech with Tim	Python, games, AI
Simplilearn	Free courses and crash tutorials

Pick one, stick with it for a month, and apply everything.

Best Communities to Ask for Help

1. Stack Overflow – Ask or search for any error
2. Reddit r/learnprogramming – Friendly for beginners
3. Discord coding servers – Get real-time help
4. GitHub – Share projects, learn from others
5. Replit Community – Show your apps, get feedback

Remember: Asking is not weakness. It's smart.

Feeling Stuck? Here's What to Do

• Try a different explanation (video, article, forum)
• Take a break, then return later
• Teach someone else what you learned—it clarifies YOUR thinking
• Build a small project to apply that concept
• Switch topics temporarily (move from Python to HTML, then back)
You don't have to learn everything at once. Take small bites.

Avoid Burnout: Take Care of Yourself

Coding is fun—but don't overdo it. Here's how to stay balanced:

Do	Don't
Take screen breaks	Code 5 hours non-stop
Go outside, move	Sit too long
Sleep well	Stay up debugging all night
Celebrate wins	Obsess over bugs

Your brain needs rest to grow.

Learning Roadmap for Teen Coders

Stage	What to Learn
1. Basics	Python or block coding
2. Projects	Games, quizzes, tools
3. Web Dev	HTML, CSS, JavaScript
4. Career Skills	GitHub, problem solving
5. Advanced	AI, APIs, frameworks
6. Internships	Real-world coding experience

Choose your pace. Don't rush. Depth > speed.

Real Teen Success Stories

- **Tanvi (17):** Learned Python on YouTube, now builds bots for her school.
- **Anuj (16):** Finished freeCodeCamp's web dev course, freelances simple websites.
- **Ritika (15):** Built a portfolio of 4 projects and got an internship at a coding bootcamp.

They all started where you are now. What made them stand out? They kept going.

Chapter Recap

Let's wrap up what you've learned:

- Smart learning = clear goals, daily practice, active building
- Start with free resources; level up when ready
- Code along, ask questions, build projects
- Join communities and share your work
- Don't compare—learn at your own pace
- Avoid burnout—rest is part of the process

Quick Quiz

1. What's the best way to avoid burnout while coding?
2. Name two free platforms to learn coding online.
3. Why is "code along" better than "just watching"?
4. What's one sign you're learning actively?
5. What should you do when stuck on a coding problem?

Final Activity: Design Your Personal Learning Plan

Create your custom 4-week plan:
- **Week 1:**
- **Week 2:**
- **Week 3:**
- **Week 4:**

Choose platforms, projects, and daily time (e.g., 30 mins/day). Share it with a friend or family member to stay accountable.

Remember: You don't need to rush. You just need to start smart.

Chapter 10

Careers in Coding and Computer Science

Introduction: Your Code, Your Career

What if your love for coding could become your career? Whether you're into building apps, solving puzzles, designing games, or fighting cybercrime—there's a tech job waiting for you.

The world is changing fast, and coders are in high demand. In this chapter,

you'll explore:

- 8 exciting careers in coding and tech
- The skills, tools, and learning paths for each
- A peek into a day in the life of tech pros
- Tips to get started while you're still in school

Get ready to discover where your coding journey could take you!

1. Software Developer

What They Do:
Build applications, programs, and tools that we use every day—on computers, phones, and tablets.

Common Tools:
- **Languages:** Python, Java, C++
- **IDEs:** Visual Studio, IntelliJ
- **Version Control:** Git & GitHub

Day in the Life:
Write and test code, fix bugs, attend team meetings, update features, document programs.

Skills Needed:
Problem-solving, strong logic, teamwork, attention to detail.

Start Here:
- Learn Python and Java
- Build simple apps and tools (e.g., to-do list, calculator)
- Contribute to open-source on GitHub

2. Web Developer (Frontend + Backend)

What They Do:
Build websites—everything from how it looks (frontend) to how it works (backend).

Frontend Stack:
HTML, CSS, JavaScript, React

Backend Stack:
Node.js, Python (Django/Flask), databases (SQL, MongoDB)

Day in the Life:
Design and update websites, ensure mobile compatibility, connect frontend to backend.

Skills Needed:
Creativity, responsive design, API knowledge, teamwork.

Start Here:
• Build your own portfolio site
• Clone a simple website (Netflix, Amazon homepage)
• Learn Git, CSS frameworks (like Bootstrap)

3. Game Developer

What They Do:
Design and code games—from mobile puzzles to 3D PC adventures.

Tools of the Trade:
Unity (C#), Unreal Engine (C++), Blender (for design), Godot

Day in the Life:
Work with designers to create levels, fix bugs, optimize performance, test user experience.

Skills Needed:
Creative thinking, math/physics, storytelling, debugging.

Start Here:
• Make a simple game in Scratch or Python (like Tic Tac Toe or Snake)
• Learn Unity basics
• Join game jams or online game contests

4. Cybersecurity Analyst

What They Do:
Protect systems, websites, and data from hackers and threats.

Tools:
Wireshark, Kali Linux, firewalls, ethical hacking software

Day in the Life:
Test for vulnerabilities, monitor threats, fix security flaws, create safety protocols.

Skills Needed:
Curiosity, attention to detail, problem-solving, basic networking.

Start Here:
- Learn basics of networks and operating systems
- Try ethical hacking courses (CEH)
- Use platforms like TryHackMe or Hack The Box

5. Data Scientist

What They Do:
Use code + math to understand patterns in big data and make smart decisions.

Common Tools:
Python, R, SQL, pandas, NumPy, matplotlib, Jupyter

Day in the Life:
Clean and analyze data, create models, visualize results, help businesses decide what to do next.

Skills Needed:
Math (statistics), logic, storytelling with data, Python

Start Here:
• Analyze your school's exam scores in Python
• Learn to use pandas and matplotlib
• Try beginner data projects (Netflix trends, weather data)

6. AI/ML Engineer

What They Do:
Build smart machines and models that learn—like chatbots, recommendation engines, or face detection.

Tools:
Python, TensorFlow, Keras, scikit-learn, OpenCV

Day in the Life:
Train machine learning models, test predictions, fine-tune performance, work with data teams.

Skills Needed:
Strong Python, algebra, data handling, logical reasoning

Start Here:
• Use Teachable Machine to build a mini AI
• Learn basics of ML with scikit-learn
• Build a chatbot or sentiment analyzer

7. App Developer (Android/iOS)

What They Do:
Create apps for smartphones and tablets.

Languages/Tools:
Java, Kotlin (Android), Swift (iOS), Flutter (cross-platform), Android Studio, Firebase

Day in the Life:
Code app features, test on devices, upload updates, fix bugs, improve design.

Skills Needed:
Mobile UI/UX knowledge, API integration, problem-solving, debugging

Start Here:
- Try MIT App Inventor
- Learn Flutter or Kotlin
- Create simple apps (counter, daily planner, quote of the day)

8. Entrepreneur / Tech Startup Founder

What They Do:
Use tech and coding to build their own product or company (like Zomato, Ola, or BYJU'S)

Tools:
Depends on the idea! Could include web tools, app platforms, or AI APIs

Day in the Life:
Code + manage business, build team, pitch to investors, test product, solve real-world problems.

Skills Needed:
Coding + leadership + creativity + risk-taking

Start Here:
- Build a simple app or website to solve a school/local problem
- Learn how to pitch ideas
- Join startup clubs or innovation events (like Atal Tinkering Labs)

Comparing Coding Careers

Career	Coding Focus	Fun Factor	Earning Potential
Software Dev	Apps & tools	☆☆☆☆	₹₹₹₹
Web Dev	Websites	☆☆☆☆	₹₹₹
Game Dev	Games & animation	☆☆☆☆☆	₹₹₹
Cybersecurity	Online safety	☆☆☆☆	₹₹₹₹
Data Science	Math + patterns	☆☆☆	₹₹₹₹
AI/ML	Smart systems	☆☆☆☆	₹₹₹₹₹
App Dev	Mobile apps	☆☆☆☆	₹₹₹
Startup Founder	Anything!	☆☆☆☆☆	Unlimited

How to Start Preparing Now

Even if you're in school, here's how to start:

Learn:
• Python, HTML/CSS, basic JS
• Logic building, problem solving
• GitHub and project sharing

Build:
• Projects for fun or school (quiz app, calculator, portfolio site)
• Try mini-internships or online competitions (hackathons, AI4Youth, coding olympiads)

Share:
• Make a GitHub profile
• Join tech forums and student communities
• Create a digital resume with your projects

Interview with a Teen Coder

Name: Zoya Mehta (Age 17)
Goal: Become an AI Engineer

Q: How did you start?
I started with Python during lockdown. Then I built a chatbot that replies to questions about planets.

Q: Where do you learn from?
YouTube channels like Apna College and projects from GitHub.

Q: What's your dream?
To build an AI system that helps students study smarter.
Advice to others:

"Don't wait till college—start building now, even if it's small."

Career Preparation Tips

Action	Why It Helps
Build projects	Shows real skills
Join school coding clubs	Practice + collaboration
Take part in hackathons	Learn under pressure
Create a LinkedIn profile	Get discovered early
Ask teachers/mentors	Learn from experience

Bonus: Get Ready for Internships & Competitions

- Join school clubs (robotics, STEM, coding)
- Attend webinars, workshops (AI4Youth, Tinker Fest, etc.)

- **Participate in:**
    - o Google Code-In
    - o Technothlon
    - o Atal Innovation Challenge
    - o Smart India Hackathon
    - o TCS CodeVita

Keep certificates, project links, and write-ups ready in a portfolio file.

Chapter Recap

Let's summarize this power-packed chapter:

• Coding opens doors to software, AI, web, games, security, and startups
• Each career needs different tools, but all start with logic + creativity
• You can prepare now through projects, platforms, and competitions
• Explore, experiment, and stay curious—your dream tech job is waiting!

Quick Quiz

1. What does a Data Scientist do?
2. Name one tool a Web Developer uses.
3. What's the difference between frontend and backend?
4. How can you start preparing for a tech career in school?
5. What kind of projects can you add to your GitHub?

Final Activity: Match Your Interests to Careers

What You Like	Matching Career
Drawing and Design	Frontend Web Dev or Game Dev
Solving puzzles	Cybersecurity Analyst
Math and stats	Data Scientist or AI Engineer
Talking to people	Tech Entrepreneur
Playing games	Game Developer or App Developer

Now write your answer:

- The tech career I'm most excited about: __________
- Why it suits me: ___________________________
- What I'll do this week to move toward it: __________

Chapter 11

Girls Who Code & Everyone Can Code

Introduction: Coding Has No Gender

Can girls code?

Can non-engineers build apps?

Can kids learn to automate things?

Absolutely.

The truth is simple: Coding is for everyone. No matter your gender, age, background, or marks in math, if you're curious and love to build things, the world of programming is wide open to you.

This chapter will break stereotypes, celebrate women in tech, and empower YOU—girl or boy, city or village—to say: Yes, I can code!

Breaking the Stereotypes

You may have heard:
- "Coding is for boys."
- "Girls don't like computers."
- "You need to be a genius to code."

These myths are false. In fact:
- Some of the world's first computer programmers were women.
- Girls who code often outperform boys in logic and design.
- You don't need to be a genius. You just need to start.

The only real requirement? Interest + effort.

The Truth About Learning to Code

Myth	Truth
You need to be a math expert	You just need logical thinking
Coding is only for engineers	Kids, artists, even writers code today
Girls aren't good at tech	Girls are leading tech in every field
You need expensive gadgets	You can start on a phone or low-cost laptop

Coding is about ideas, curiosity, and creativity—qualities that everyone has.

Girls Who Changed the World with Code

Let's meet some inspiring Indian women who are coding their way to success:

Richa Kar – Founder of Zivame

What she built: India's leading online lingerie brand
How tech helped: She used data analytics and coding tools to study buying patterns and launched a user-friendly e-commerce site.

Suchi Mukherjee – Founder of Limeroad
What she built: A fashion discovery platform powered by smart tech
How tech helped: Created an app that allows users to design and shop stylish looks using AI-powered suggestions.

Bhavishya Goel – App Developer at 16
What she built: A school event tracking app
How tech helped: She learned app development on YouTube, used MIT App Inventor, and built something useful for her entire school.

Reshma Saujani – Founder of Girls Who Code (USA)
What she built: A global movement to help girls learn programming
How tech helped: Started with one coding club. Now there are thousands worldwide.

Why We Need More Girls in Tech

- Only 1 in 5 tech professionals in India are women
- More girls = more ideas, better products
- Women bring empathy, creativity, and collaboration—perfect for coding
- NEP 2020 now encourages digital and coding skills for all genders in schools

By learning to code, girls can:
- Earn respect
- Gain independence
- Lead innovation
- Shape India's digital future

Role of Teachers & Parents

Parents and teachers must support girls by:

- Providing equal access to computers and STEM kits
- Encouraging them to join tech clubs, hackathons
- Praising effort, not just results
- Being patient and positive role models

Remember: Confidence comes from support.

How Schools Can Support Everyone to Code

Under the National Education Policy (NEP) 2020, schools are now encouraged to:

- Start coding from Grades 6 onwards
- Create coding clubs (CoC) for hands-on learning
- Include coding in Bagless Days and Activity Periods
- Use tools like Scratch, Python, HTML/CSS, and App Inventor
- Bring in local tech role models to inspire students

India's Programs Supporting Girl Coders

Initiative	**What It Offers**
AI for Youth (CBSE + Intel)	Free AI basics, coding tools, projects
Girls in Tech – NASSCOM	Scholarships and mentorship
Atal Innovation Mission (NITI Aayog)	Tinkering Labs in schools
Digital India Mission	Internet + digital skills training
She Codes India Hackathons	Coding contests for girls in school and college

Explore them, participate, and shine!

Real-Life Teen Girl Coders

Aarya (Age 15) – Built a Chatbot
"I made a Python chatbot for my school library. Now students can ask it for book suggestions!"

Neha (Age 13) – Scratch Game Developer
"I designed a game where a girl saves the environment. My friends loved it and asked me to teach them Scratch too!"

Ananya (Age 16) – Web Designer
"I made a portfolio website for my aunt's art business. She started getting more customers!"

You don't need a degree to start—you just need a dream.

Everyone Can Code – Boys Too!

Coding isn't just for girls either—it's for everyone.

Boys should support and collaborate with girl coders. Together, we can:

- Build inclusive teams
- Learn diverse ways of thinking
- Celebrate each other's successes
- Make the tech world kind and creative

Let's move from "me vs. you" to "we build together."

Clubs and Communities to Join

Name	Who It's For	What It Offers
Girls Who Code (India Chapters)	School girls	Free courses, mentors, clubs
CodeChef for Schools	Boys and girls	Weekly challenges, leaderboard
Scratch Community	Kids 8–16	Share games and animations
She Loves Code Discord Server	Girls 13+	Supportive coding chat rooms
AI4Youth Clubs	CBSE school students	AI projects + certification

Search for your nearest chapter or start your own club!

Career Paths for Girl Coders

Interest	Career Option
Drawing / design	UI/UX Designer, Web Dev
Teaching	Coding Trainer, Tech Educator
Science + logic	AI Engineer, Data Scientist
Security / mystery	Cybersecurity Analyst
Problem-solving	Software Developer, App Builder
Storytelling	Game Developer, Animator

Tech isn't one path—it's many. Pick yours!

Tools That Make Coding Fun & Friendly

Tool	Why It's Great
Scratch	Easy to start with, drag & drop blocks
MIT App Inventor	Build real mobile apps without typing code
Code.org	Beginner-friendly with game-based learning
Replit	Write Python and HTML in the browser
Canva + AI	Design and code smart presentations, logos

Start with what's fun—and grow from there.

Action Plan: Get Started in 5 Steps

1. Pick a language or platform (e.g., Scratch or Python)
2. Choose a project (e.g., quiz game, story website)
3. Block 30 minutes daily to practice
4. Join a coding group or club
5. Ask for help when needed—never be afraid to learn

Chapter Recap

Let's review what we've explored:

- Coding is for girls, boys, everyone
- Myths like "coding is for boys" are outdated and false
- Many inspiring Indian women are leading tech today
- Schools, parents, and friends can support more girls in tech
- Start with simple tools, join clubs, and build real projects
- Empowered teens—of all genders—can lead India's tech future

Quick Quiz

1. Name one Indian woman who founded a tech company.
2. What is Scratch used for?
3. What does NEP 2020 say about coding in schools?
4. What kind of projects have teen girls built?
5. How can boys support inclusive tech spaces?

Final Activity: Reflect and Plan

Answer these:

- One myth about coding I used to believe: ____________
- One girl in tech who inspires me: ____________
- My first project idea: ______________
- What I'll do this week: ______________
- Who will I invite to code with me: ______________

Remember: You belong in tech. Let's build the future together.

Chapter 12

Build Your First Portfolio

Introduction: : Your Work Speaks Louder Than Marks

Imagine you're applying for an internship, tech club, or even college. What's the one thing that can make you stand out from the crowd? Your coding portfolio.

A portfolio is your digital treasure chest. It shows your:

- Projects
- Skills
- Interests
- Growth journey

Whether you're a beginner or budding coder, this chapter will guide you to build a powerful tech portfolio—step by step."

What Is a Coding Portfolio?

A coding portfolio is a collection of your work that showcases what you can build, solve, or create using code. It's like a resume—but way more exciting!

It can include:

- Web pages you've built
- Python projects
- Games and animations
- AI experiments
- Apps you designed
- School IT projects

And the best part? Even if you're still learning, you can start NOW.

Why Do You Need One in School?

Reason	**Why It Matters**
Shows your real skills	More than just marks
Global exposure	Can share with mentors or colleges
Builds confidence	You see how much you've grown
Internship-ready	Start applying early
Stands out in competitions	Judges love seeing work in action

What to Include in Your Portfolio

Let's break it down:

1. Introduction

- Name, grade, school
- A short paragraph about your interests (e.g., "I love building Python

tools and designing websites!")

2. Projects (the heart of your portfolio)

Include 3–5 projects with:

• Title (e.g., "To-Do List Web App")
• Screenshot or demo video
• Tech used (Python, HTML, Scratch)
• What it does
• What YOU learned or built

3. Skills List

• **Languages:** Python, HTML, JavaScript
• **Tools:** Replit, GitHub, Scratch, Canva
• **Soft Skills:** teamwork, creativity, presentation

4. Certifications (if any)

• Coding Ninja badge
• Code.org certificate
• Google CS First, AI4Youth, etc.

5. Contact Info

• Email or LinkedIn
• GitHub username
• **Optional:** your blog or YouTube if you explain coding

How to Build Your Portfolio (Step-by-Step)

Let's build it together!

Step 1: Choose a Format

You can create your portfolio in one of these ways:

Method	Tools
Website	HTML/CSS or portfolio builders like Wix, Carrd
GitHub Repo	Code + readme files
Google Slides	Easy to present visually
PDF / Canva	Stylish for quick sharing
Blog / Notion Page	Interactive and flexible

Pick one that feels easy to start with. You can upgrade later.

Step 2: Select Projects
Choose 3–5 of your best/favorite projects. Mix it up:

Type	Example
Web Dev	Your personal website
Python	Calculator, quiz, chatbot
Scratch	Animation or game
AI/ML	Sentiment analyzer or Teachable Machine
App	Planner built with MIT App Inventor

Even small projects count. Just make sure YOU made them.

Step 3: Write Project Descriptions

Use this easy format:
Title: Weather Forecast App
Built With: HTML, CSS, JavaScript
What It Does: Shows the current weather using OpenWeather API
What I Learned: How APIs work, designing user interfaces
Keep it short, honest, and specific.

Step 4: Add Screenshots or Links

A good portfolio SHOWS, not just TELLS.

Add:
• Screenshots of your code or interface
• GIFs of your app running
• Video demos (you can upload to Google Drive or YouTube)
• GitHub link to the code

Tip: Keep your project files well-organized in folders.

Step 5: Add Your "About Me"

Write a short, punchy introduction. Examples:
• "Hi! I'm Kabir, a 10th grader who loves Python and building fun games."
• "I enjoy solving problems with code, designing simple websites, and learning AI tools."
Use emojis or icons if it's a website—keep it fun!

Where to Host Your Portfolio

Platform	Why Use It
GitHub Pages	Free hosting for HTML portfolios
Carrd	Simple drag-and-drop websites
Replit	Showcase and run code in the browser
Notion	Share a beautiful single-page profile
LinkedIn	Use the "Featured" section to pin your projects

All About GitHub

GitHub is the best place to host your code.
Here's how to get started:
Step-by-Step:
1. Create a free GitHub account

2. Create a new repository (repo)
3. Upload your project files
4. Write a README.md (explains your project)
5. Share the link!

Tip: Write your README like a blog post—with a title, features, screenshots, and "how to use."

Sample Portfolio: Meet Arjun, Grade 11

About Me:
I'm Arjun, a student from Delhi who loves coding, cricket, and creating tech for fun.

Projects:
1. Quiz Game in Python
   – Built with loops and if-else
   – Helps friends study for exams
2. Eco-Reminder Web App
   – Built using HTML, CSS, JS
   – Sends pop-up alerts to turn off lights
3. Tic Tac Toe Game (Scratch)
   – Designed for younger cousins
   – Learned how to use variables and logic blocks

Certifications:
• **AI for Youth:** Beginner
• W3Schools HTML course
GitHub: github.com/arjun-codes
Email: arjunstudent@gmail.com

Resume Tips for Tech Teens

When you're ready to apply for an internship, competition, or college tech club, add:

- Short bio
- Your top 3 projects
- Your GitHub or Replit links
- School grade + coding languages
- **Soft skills:** teamwork, presentations

Remember: Real skills + projects >>> high marks alone!

Building Blocks of a Good Portfolio

Clear, honest descriptions
Variety of projects
Easy-to-read format
Proof of skills (certificates, links)
Updated regularly
Don't worry about being perfect. Start small, build slowly.

Where to Share Your Portfolio

- With teachers during school project fairs
- During online coding competitions
- On LinkedIn or student Discord groups
- In hackathons or tech meetups
- While applying for workshops or internships

Even if you're just 15–16, people LOVE seeing motivated learners.

Bonus: Add a Personal Touch

Ideas to make your portfolio stand out:
- Add your drawing/designs (if UI/UX is your thing)
- Write a blog about your coding journey
- Share behind-the-scenes of how you fixed a tricky bug
- Add a section "What I want to learn next…"

Your portfolio = your voice.

Chapter Recap

Let's wrap it up:

• A portfolio showcases what you've built—not just what you know
• Even beginners can start one with just a few projects
• Use tools like GitHub, Google Slides, or Notion
• Include your intro, project details, skills, and screenshots
• Keep it updated and share it confidently!

Start today—build as you learn. Your future self will thank you.

Quick Quiz

1. What is the purpose of a coding portfolio?
2. Name 3 things to include in a project description.
3. What platform can you use to host your code?
4. How can you make your portfolio stand out?
5. Why is it useful to have a portfolio before college?

Final Activity: Make a Mini Portfolio (Now!)

Try this:

• Pick ONE project you've built
• Open Google Slides or Notion

• **Add:**
    o Title
    o What it does
    o Screenshot
    o What you learned

Share it with your teacher or a friend. You're now officially a coder with a portfolio!

Chapter 13

From Hobby to Career

Your Tech Journey

Introduction: From Code to Career

You started coding for fun. Maybe you built a game, solved a puzzle, or just played around with Scratch.

But now you're wondering—can I turn this into a real career?
The answer is a big YES!

In this chapter, we'll show you:
• How to turn coding from a passion into a profession
• Education paths after Class 12
• Government support and real-world opportunities
• How to plan your tech journey—step by step
Let's take your hobby to the next level!

Step 1: Know Your Options After School

When you finish Class 12, you have many ways to continue your tech journey. Based on your interest and stream (Science, Commerce, Arts), here are some common options:

For Science Stream Students

Course	What It Offers
B.Tech (Computer Science, AI/ ML, IT)	Deep dive into programming, systems, networks, AI
B.Sc. in Computer Science or Data Science	Theory + practical coding and research
B.Tech in Information Security or IoT	For cybersecurity, robotics, and smart tech careers

For Commerce/Arts Students (Yes, you too!)

Course	What It Offers
BCA (Bachelor of Computer Applications)	Focused coding + software building
Diploma in Web/App Development	Quick job-ready skills
BA/BCom + Certificate in Coding	Combine creativity with tech through short courses

Tip: You don't have to be an engineer to be a coder.

Step 2: Build Skills While in School

Start now. You don't need to wait till college. Do these:

- Learn Python, HTML/CSS, or JavaScript
- Build 2–3 simple projects

• Take a free course on Coursera or YouTube
• Join your school's coding or STEM club
• Make a basic portfolio using GitHub or Google Slides

Every project = One step toward your career.

Step 3: Explore Government Programs That Support You
India is building a digital-first future—and you're part of it!
Here are key initiatives helping students like you:

Digital India Mission

Aim: Make India digitally empowered
What You Get:
• Free online learning portals
• More coding labs in schools
• Public Wi-Fi, eBooks, and eLearning tools

Atal Innovation Mission (AIM)

Run by: NITI Aayog

What You Get:
• Atal Tinkering Labs (ATLs) in schools
• Robotic kits, coding tools, maker spaces
• Support for student innovations
• Contests like ATL Marathon and TinkerFest

Skill India + PMKVY

What You Get:
• Free skill-based tech training
• Certification in IT tools, app building
• Support for jobs and entrepreneurship

Visit: www.skillindia.gov.in

AI For Youth (by CBSE + Intel)

What You Get:

- Learn AI, data, and Python basics
- Build projects using real-world datasets
- Certificate after training
- Chance to present ideas globally

Join through your school or district portal!

Step 4: Aim for Hackathons, Olympiads, and Internships

Even as a school student, you can enter competitions that colleges and tech companies respect.

Program	For Whom	Benefits
Smart India Hackathon (SIH)	Classes 9–12 & college	National exposure, cash prizes
Google Code-In / GSoC	Teens worldwide	Real coding tasks in open source
National Coding Olympiad (Coding Ninjas)	School students	Competitive programming
TCS iON Career Edge	High schoolers	Free career skills programs
Internships in startups	16+ age	Hands-on experience

Win or lose—you learn either way.

Step 5: Possible Career Paths in Tech

Once you build your skills and projects, you can work in:

Career	What You'll Do
Software Developer	Build apps, games, platforms
Web Developer	Design websites, user interfaces
AI/ML Engineer	Work on smart machines, predictions
Cybersecurity Analyst	Protect systems from hackers
Data Scientist	Analyze big data to find trends
Game Developer	Build gaming logic, design gameplay
App Developer	Create mobile tools and experiences
Tech Educator	Teach others coding and tech

Some of these need degrees. Some just need skills + projects + passion.

Step 6: What Recruiters and Colleges Look For

Whether you apply for a college seat, tech internship, or future job, **here's what decision-makers want:**

What They Check	Why It Matters
Projects	Real proof of learning
Problem-Solving	Logical, creative thinking
Communication	Can explain tech in simple terms
Collaboration	Can work in teams
Continuous Learning	Learns new tools quickly

Grades help. But skills + portfolio win.

Famous Tech Colleges in India

Here are top institutes for a tech career:

- IITs – B.Tech, M.Tech in CS/AI
- NITs – National Institutes of Technology
- IIITs – Top for Information Tech
- BITS Pilani / VIT / SRM / Amity – Leading private tech schools
- IGNOU / DU / BHU / IPU – Offer BCA & short-term CS programs

Many of these accept students from all streams with basic coding interest.

Scholarships and Free Courses

Don't let money stop your dreams. Explore:

Name	Who Can Apply	What You Get
Google India Scholarships	Girls in STEM	Free training, mentorship
NSP (National Scholarship Portal)	All students	Govt. funding for degrees
Coursera for Campus	Partnered schools	Free access to coding courses
Code.org / Khan Academy	Anyone	100% free coding curriculum
NPTEL (IIT courses)	School & college	Free + certified courses on tech topics

Ask your school to partner with these platforms.

Real-World Success Stories

Raj, 17 – Built a News App

Raj used JavaScript and APIs to build an app that fetches daily news headlines. He shared it on GitHub and got internship offers!

Meera, 16 – Interned at a Startup
Meera joined a local coding workshop and impressed a startup mentor. She now helps them test features as a part-time intern.

Aarav, 18 – Became a Coding Mentor
Aarav made YouTube videos explaining Python basics to school kids. He now teaches at a coding club and earns on the side.

Your Roadmap – Plan Your Journey

Here's a simple checklist:

1. Start learning coding basics (Python, HTML)
2. Build your first 2–3 mini projects
3. Join a coding club or online community
4. Participate in 1 competition or hackathon
5. Explore short-term certified courses
6. Create your portfolio
7. Decide post-Class 12 path (degree or diploma)
8. Apply for internships or workshops

Start small. Stay consistent. One project at a time.

Chapter Recap

Let's wrap up what we learned:

- You can turn your love for coding into a full-fledged career
- There are many paths: B.Tech, BCA, Diplomas, and short courses
- Government programs like AIM and Digital India support young coders
- Hackathons, Olympiads, and internships boost your journey
- Start early, learn continuously, and build your portfolio

Your coding hobby isn't just fun—it's your future career ticket.

Quick Quiz

1. What are two career paths for coders after Class 12?
2. What is the Atal Innovation Mission?
3. Name one scholarship program for students in tech.
4. Why is a portfolio more important than marks?
5. How can you prepare for a tech job or college from school?

Final Activity: Create Your Tech Career Plan

Answer these:

- What coding course will I take next month? ________________
- What kind of projects excite me the most? ________________
- What stream/degree might I consider after Class 12? _____________
- What tech career would I love to try in the future? ______________
- What's one step I'll take this week? ________________

Chapter 14

The Future of Coding

What's Next?

Introduction: Welcome to Tomorrow

You've learned to code. You've built projects. You even know about careers in tech.
But here's the big question: What's coming next?
How will coding change?
Will it become easier? Harder?
Will AI replace coders—or will it help them?

In this final chapter, we'll explore:

• Future trends in tech and coding
• New ways to build (like no-code platforms)
• Why ethics and creativity matter
• How YOU can shape the digital world ahead

Let's time-travel into the future—are you ready?

The Rise of Low-Code and No-Code Platforms

Coding is becoming more accessible. You no longer need to write 1000 lines of code to build something amazing.
That's where low-code and no-code platforms come in.

What Are They?

• Low-code = You write some code, but also use visual tools (drag-and-drop blocks, templates)
• No-code = You use pre-built tools and logic—no actual code written

Examples

Platform	**What It Does**
MIT App Inventor	Build Android apps using blocks
Thunkable	App creation with no coding needed
Bubble.io	Build full websites and apps visually
Canva Apps	Build mini tools with AI drag-and-drop
Webflow	Create websites without code
Scratch	Kids' games and animations with blocks

Why It Matters

• Speeds up development
• Non-tech users (designers, teachers, students) can build tools
• Helps you test ideas faster
• Great for prototyping or school projects

Important: These tools don't replace coding—they help you start. To go deeper, real coding still matters.

Coding + AI = Superpowers

You've already seen how AI tools like ChatGPT, GitHub Copilot, and Teachable Machine are helping developers.
Let's go a bit deeper.

AI in Coding: What's Happening?

• AI can write code (with your guidance)
• AI can find bugs and fix them
• AI can explain code (like a teacher)
• AI can generate visuals, voices, and designs

But remember: AI needs a smart human to lead it. That's where YOU come in.

Must-Know AI Tools for Young Coders

Tool	What It Helps With
GitHub Copilot	Suggests code as you type
ChatGPT	Helps explain, debug, or write code
Teachable Machine (by Google)	Train ML models easily
Runway ML	Create AI videos and tools
Scratch + ML extensions	Use ML in simple games
Kaggle Notebooks	Learn data science hands-on

AI isn't scary. It's your coding sidekick!

Ethics in a Tech-Driven World

As technology grows, so do responsibilities.

Think of questions like:
• Should AI be allowed to decide who gets a loan?
• Can an app track everything you do without asking?
• What if a robot makes a mistake—who's responsible?

These are called ethical dilemmas, and they are the future of tech decision-making.

Principles Every Coder Should Learn

1. Data Privacy – Respect user information
2. Transparency – Show how your app works
3. Inclusion – Make tools usable for all
4. Fairness – Avoid bias in AI or decision logic
5. Accountability – Own your creations

Ethics = Integrity + Empathy + Smart Decisions
Even if you're coding for fun, build with kindness and honesty.

Soft Skills = Big Impact

In the future, the best coders won't just be good at typing.

They'll also be:
• Creative problem-solvers
• Effective communicators
• Critical thinkers
• Empathetic team players
• Ethical decision-makers
The "soft" skills will become the "super" skills.

Open Source: Code Together, Grow Together

Want to level up fast? Join the open-source movement.

Open source means:

- Projects where anyone can read, use, or contribute to the code
- Communities that grow by sharing knowledge
- Tools that are free, powerful, and used worldwide

Famous Open-Source Tools

Tool	What It Does
Linux	Operating system powering servers
Firefox	Web browser
WordPress	Website builder
TensorFlow	AI/ML library
VS Code	Code editor
Python	Yes, even Python is open source!

You can contribute even as a teen:

- Fix bugs
- Translate documentation
- Suggest UI ideas
- Create tutorials

Tip: Start by exploring on GitHub. Look for “good first issue” tags.

Startups & Entrepreneurship

Love building new ideas? You might be a future tech founder. India’s startup scene is booming—and young minds are part of it!

Young Techpreneurs to Know

- Shravan and Sanjay Kumaran – Built apps at age 12
- Harshwardhans & Tanmay Bakshi – AI experts before 18
- Ritesh Agarwal (OYO Rooms) – Started with coding at 17

You don't need a huge office. **You need:**

- An idea
- A team
- A working demo
- Passion

Platforms like Startup India and Tinkerpreneur Bootcamp help school students start early.

Your Place in a Digital-First World

The future world needs:

Role	**Skill Needed**
Digital Designers	Code + creativity
AI Thinkers	Logic + ethics
Tech Communicators	Code + storytelling
App Builders	UX + backend
Tech-for-Good Leaders	Code + social impact

Whatever your strength—design, logic, writing, planning—you can shape tomorrow.

Experiment: Your "Future-Ready" Challenge

Try this:
Imagine a future where every home has a robot helper.
What would you want it to do?
How would it learn?
What if it made a mistake?
Write a short app idea or flowchart for it.

This is how top innovators think!

Bonus: 5 Future Trends to Watch

1. Quantum Computing – Beyond 0s and 1s!
2. Bioinformatics – Code + biology = disease-fighting tools
3. Metaverse – Build digital worlds
4. EdTech & AI Tutors – Personalized learning
5. Smart Cities – IoT + data for better lives

Stay curious. Read blogs. Watch TED Talks. Ask "what's next?"

Chapter Recap

Let's rewind:

- Coding is evolving into visual, AI-supported, ethical, and collaborative fields
- No-code/low-code makes building faster and easier
- AI is your co-coder, not your competition
- Ethics, open source, and creativity matter as much as logic
- The digital world is waiting for YOU to lead it!

Quick Quiz

1. What is a no-code platform?
2. Name one ethical issue in AI or coding.
3. What is open source?
4. What skills do you need to be a tech entrepreneur?
5. How can AI help you code better?

Abeer's Coding Insight
You don't need to master every language. Focus on learning how to think like a developer — the languages will change, but logic stays.

Final Activity: Design Your "2035" Career Poster

- Job Title: ______________________

- What I'll Build: ______________________
- Tools I'll Use: ______________________
- My Superpower Skill: ______________________
- What Will Change Because of Me:

Print it. Stick it. Dream it. Live it.

Glossary

50 Coding Terms Simplified

1.	**Algorithm** – A step-by-step set of instructions to solve a problem.
2.	**API (Application Programming Interface)** – A tool that lets different apps talk to each other.
3.	**Array** – A list of items stored in a single variable.
4.	**Artificial Intelligence (AI)** – When computers can do tasks that usually need human smarts.
5.	**Backend** – The part of a website/app that users don't see (data, logic, database).
6.	**Boolean** – A data type with two values: true or false.
7.	**Bug** – An error or problem in a code that stops it from working correctly.
8.	**Class** – A blueprint to create similar objects in object-oriented programming.
9.	**Cloud Computing** – Storing and accessing data and software over the internet.
10.	**Code** – The instructions written to make a computer do something.
11.	**Compiler** – A tool that converts code into a language the computer understands.
12.	**CSS (Cascading Style Sheets)** – Used to style HTML pages.
13.	**Data Science** – Finding patterns in data to make decisions or predictions.
14.	**Database** – A place to store organized data digitally.
15.	**Debugging** – Fixing bugs in a program.

16.	**Frontend** – The part of a website/app you can see and interact with.
17.	**Function** – A reusable block of code that does a specific task.
18.	**Git** – A tool that tracks changes in your code.
19.	**GitHub** – A website to store and share code projects.
20.	**HTML (HyperText Markup Language)** – Used to create web pages.
21.	**IDE (Integrated Development Environment)** – A coding workspace like VS Code or Thonny.
22.	**If-Else Statement** – Code that makes decisions.
23.	**Input** – Data given to a program.
24.	**JavaScript** – A language that makes websites interactive.
25.	**Library** – A collection of prewritten code for specific tasks.
26.	**Loop** – Code that repeats until a condition is met.
27.	**Low-code** – Building software using a mix of visual tools and small amounts of code.
28.	**Machine Learning (ML)** – A type of AI where computers learn from data.
29.	**Mobile App** – A software program that runs on smartphones and tablets.
30.	**No-code** – Building software without writing code.
31.	**Object** – A thing in programming that has data and functions.
32.	**Open Source** – Code that anyone can use, modify, and share freely.
33.	**Output** – What a program gives back after running (like results).
34.	**Python** – A beginner-friendly and powerful programming language.

35.	**Scratch** – A visual programming platform for kids.
36.	**Software Developer** – A person who builds programs or apps.
37.	**String** – A group of characters (letters, numbers, symbols).
38.	**Syntax** – The rules of how code must be written.
39.	**UI (User Interface)** – What users interact with on screen.
40.	**UX (User Experience)** – The experience of using a product (ease, design, feeling).
41.	**Variable** – A container to store values in code.
42.	**Version Control** – Keeping track of code changes over time.
43.	**Visual Programming** – Coding using drag-and-drop blocks instead of text.
44.	**Web Development** – Creating websites and web apps.
45.	**While Loop** – A loop that keeps running while a condition is true.
46.	**Java** – A popular language used in Android apps and enterprise software.
47.	C++ – A powerful language used in gaming and system development.
48.	**Thonny** – A beginner-friendly IDE for learning Python.
49.	**Boolean Logic** – A form of logic with true/false values, used in coding decisions.
50.	**Compiler Error** – A message you get when code has a mistake and doesn't run.

Book Summary

Key Takeaways

The Big Book of Coding for Teenagers is your go-to guide to enter the world of programming, software, and tech careers. Here's what you've explored:

Understanding the Basics

• Coding = giving instructions to a computer.
• Programming languages like Python and JavaScript help you talk to machines.
• Frontend and backend are two sides of any tech product.

Learning to Code

• You can begin with visual tools like Scratch and move to Python or HTML/CSS.
• Use IDEs like VS Code or Thonny to start coding easily.
• Best beginner sites: W3Schools, Code.org, Khan Academy.

Problem-Solving and Logic

• Break problems into steps (algorithms).
• Think logically like a computer.
• Debugging helps improve your thinking.

Build Real Stuff

• Make to-do apps, games, websites, quizzes.
• Your projects matter more than your marks.

AI, Visual Coding & Tools

• Tools like ChatGPT, GitHub Copilot, and Teachable Machine can

help you build faster.
• Low-code and no-code platforms make building apps super simple.

Career Awareness

• Roles include software developer, game designer, AI engineer, cybersecurity analyst, and more.
• Build your portfolio, join hackathons, and explore open-source projects.

Everyone Can Code

• Girls in tech, coding clubs, and school initiatives help break stereotypes.
• NEP 2020 promotes digital literacy and 21st-century skills.

Plan Your Tech Future

• Explore BCA, B.Tech, AI specializations, or even bootcamps.
• Use Digital India, Skill India, and AIM programs to boost your learning.

What's Next?

• Coding is becoming easier, faster, and more collaborative.
• Ethics, soft skills, and creative thinking will define your success.

Final Message:

You don't have to be a genius to code.
You just have to be curious, consistent, and creative.
Start small. Keep going. Your digital journey begins today!